ORIGINAL EYES

PROGRESSIVE VISION IN BRITI

Front cover
J M W TURNER
Venice: Open Air Theatre 1833

Back Cover
WOLS *Untitled* c 1944–45

PREFACE

Tate Gallery Liverpool aims to increase the appreciation, enjoyment and knowledge of twentieth century art, and despite the fact that most of the material presented here is from the eighteenth and nineteenth centuries, this exhibition has the same objective. Although the main theme is the originality of vision and technique in an earlier historical period, this theme has much to tell us about the art of our own time. We have included examples of art from the twentieth century which demonstrate sensibilities and techniques which share much with the greatest works of the past.

The art of watercolour flourished in England from 1750 to 1850 in an extraordinary way. Its greatest exponents, well represented here, demonstrated an unrivalled experimental curiosity in finding new techniques to express new ways of looking at the world. Landscape was their favoured subject because it was the field of greatest scientific and philosophical interest of the time, comparable to nuclear physics, astrophysics or genetics today. Their excitement and curiosity speak to us still through the form of their work even though their intended meaning is now obscure to all but scholars of the period. If their work seems familiar, it is because we forget how much of our world was undiscovered two hundred years ago.

Artists in our own time have likewise been engaged in discovery, and because their subjects are often challenging, the means they have used to express them seem equally so. This exhibition aims to refresh our perception of the originality of the great watercolourists at the same time as showing a continuity in visual approach between their work and the work of some of the masters of twentieth century art.

We are grateful to David Blayney Brown, a curator in the Turner Collection at Millbank, for enthusiastically accepting the unusual brief for the exhibition, for his knowledgeable selection of the watercolours and for his illuminating essay. This draws out the fascinating relation between formal techniques and meanings, and points out how these have functioned in similar ways in the earlier period and in some of the art of the twentieth century.

Although most of the exhibition is drawn from the Tate's collections, we are most grateful to the Syndics of the Fitzwilliam Museum, Cambridge, to the Visitors of the Ashmolean Museum, Oxford, to Birmingham City Art Gallery and to the other lenders who have generously agreed to make paintings available for viewing by visitors to Tate Gallery Liverpool.

Nicholas Serota, Director, Tate Gallery

Lewis Biggs, Curator, Tate Gallery Liverpool

8

Alexander Cozens, *Plate no. 8, A water-fall* from *A New Method of Assisting the Invention in Drawing Original Compositions of Landscape* c 1785, acquatint, The Trustees of the Tate Gallery (not in exhibition)

ORIGINAL EYES

Progressive Vision in British Watercolour 1750–1850

David Blayney Brown

In 1949 the recently established Institute of Contemporary Art arranged an exhibition provocatively entitled '40,000 years of modern art'. It compared primitive and modern art, to demonstrate what Herbert Read, one of the organisers, called 'the eternal recurrence of certain phenomena in art which, on their appearance, are labelled modern'. This exhibition seeks to make a similar point within a more limited compass. It assembles a personal choice of works from a single century from about 1750, from one country, Britain, and in one medium, watercolour, and it attempts to demonstrate in them characteristics which anticipate some aspects of the modern sensibility. There is no suggestion that these works 'explain' Picasso or Matisse, Mondrian or Rothko. No direct links can be made between these artists, or others in the modern pantheon, and those from the earlier period shown here. Nor can the conceptual and technical characteristics displayed in this exhibition wholly account for the art of our time. But they may open our eyes to certain ways of seeing and representing that have been further explored by the moderns.

There is much in modern art that is neither new nor intrinsically forbidding, though popular mythology still sometimes finds it so. It would be hard to identify anything in the history of art more anodyne and 'safe' than the English watercolour as it is often imagined. But such a view is as unfair to English watercolour at its finest as are many of the more hostile conceptions of twentieth century art. This alone would be reason enough for choosing this particular territory from an enormous field, when many others would have demonstrated continuity – Read's 'eternal recurrence' – just as well. It is especially interesting to identify features in an art so popularly acceptable, that seem sometimes unacceptable or 'difficult' when developed by other means today.

There are other reasons for locating this exhibition where we have. Much happened in art and artistic theory in the second half of the eighteenth and the first half of the nineteenth century that is relevant to the twentieth. Abstraction itself is as old as man. General principles of composition or form extrapolated from memory and experience, the essence of abstraction, appear in the cave paintings of Lascaux or the sculpture of the Cyclades. But they were given a philosophical legitimacy in the eighteenth century by thinkers like Edmund Burke and artists like Alexander Cozens who acknowledged that 'general ideas' could reflect or stimulate particular sensations and moods.

Emotion was permitted to motivate the subject and execution of art as never before, and there was a new freedom to create types of subject outside established hierarchies. The almost hackneyed popularity of Thomas Rowlandson today should not blind us to the fact that his robust, British caricature was completely new, especially when combined, as in the example shown here (p 7), with sensitive depiction of landscape; and the sinister imaginings of John Hamilton Mortimer – cousins to Rowlandson's drawings in their sinuous pen line – revealed their creator's psychological state with exceptional frankness (p 7).

Two aesthetic theories, the 'Sublime' and the 'Picturesque', were developed during this period. The 'Sublime' relished the dramatic or actually frightening rather than the merely beautiful, and sent artists into the mountains of Wales or Switzerland to experience the most awe-inspiring and spectacular manifestations of nature. The 'Picturesque' concentrated on random and haphazard forms of rustic nature, and endowed the familiar, the ordinary and even the ugly with a new integrity. Both theories involved a highly selective vision, and engaged artists in an active rather than a passive relationship with the world around them, leading away from the traditional concepts of ideal beauty and perfection of finish towards more spontaneous and expressive execution, and away from the humanist values celebrated since the Renaissance towards greater emphasis on aspects of the natural world.

Such trends contributed most to the development of landscape, but had implications for all branches of

JOHN BAPTIST MALCHAIR
St Barnabus, Oxford, from the Artist's Window 1782

art. Romantic artists made their relationship to the natural world and to things that man had created a matter of constant and creative speculation. Theirs was an age of naturalism, when a mood of empiricism, a taste for 'Picturesque' ordinariness or sometimes a religious belief in the world as a manifestation of the divine, deserving of faithful study as an act of witness, moved artists to abandon more classically acceptable subjects and compositions. The Oxford drawing master J B Malchair and the young London landscapist John Linnell, for instance, produced modest renderings of backyards that would never before have been the proper business of art (above & p 9). From such views of familiar and unexceptional places, it may seem a long leap to Avigdor Arikha's painstaking scrutiny of his own painting materials (p 8), but the humble objectivity, the turning away from the conventionally pictorial, the acceptance of things as they are, was no less distinctive in its day.

Towards the end of our period, such refreshingly uncritical enquiries were joined by scientific investigation of particular forms and phenomena. Constable's sky studies (p 11), or John Ruskin's geological researches in the Alps represent yet another new approach. Constable had declared his belief in a 'natural painture' and Ruskin sought to link his art to a wider comprehension of natural order. Yet their writings reveal their strong emotional responses – in Ruskin's case a deepening pessimism before the workings of nature, and in Constable's a grateful acknowledgement of the providence of Creation, as when he inscribed his bold drawing of clouds with the lines from Robert Bloomfield's *Farmer's Boy* that compare them with 'a flock at rest' that 'aloud proclaim/Their mighty shepherd's everlasting name'. Constable's image is as emphatic and concentrated in its engagement with weather – and as charged with feeling – as Arnulf Rainer's 'Rain' (p 10).

This was also a period in which artists claimed a

THOMAS ROWLANDSON
Landscape, Isle of Wight c 1782

JOHN HAMILTON MORTIMER
Monsters c 1770s

AVIGDOR ARIKHA
Tubes of Paint in their Drawer 1985

PAUL KLEE
They're Biting 1920

JOHN LINNELL
Tatham's Garden, Alpha Road, at Evening 1812

ARNULF RAINER
Rain 1951

JOHN CONSTABLE
Cloud Study with Verses from [Robert] Bloomfield c 1830s

new freedom to look back into the art of the past for stylistic examples that seemed best to serve their purpose and correspond to their emotions irrespective of whether the examples they chose were fashionable or familiar. Mortimer looked to the grotesques of Salvator Rosa or Jacques Callot for his tormented monsters, but others like Blake and Samuel Palmer found the most impressive analogues of their own intense emotions in the 'primitive' art of the later middle ages and early Renaissance. They looked to these archaic types in European art for a language of expression in much the same spirit as artists from Gauguin to Paul Klee (p 8) have looked to the South Seas, the Cyclades or Africa.

These necessarily random glimpses of a complex period may help to suggest at least some of its relevance to our own age. The readiness to question the nature of reality, or to abstract or generalise from it, the interest in natural rather than humanist values, the abandonment of beauty as an end in itself, the belief in sense-impressions and emotions that we find in the art of this century, and may sometimes find difficult, can all be found in this earlier period. But why Britain, and why watercolour? It is no exaggeration to say that the most outstanding British watercolourists were then the most advanced and original artists in Europe. In both conception and technique they were breaking entirely new ground. Theirs was the 'new art' of their day, the driving force for a fresh and immediate vision of the world, or for the expression of the workings of the imagination, that was widely recognised for its modernity. Their technical achievements alone marked them out, and set them at the forefront of a national school that was itself far ahead of its competitors. Surveying the state of the arts in 1855, at the end of our period, the critic Théophile Gautier wrote this of British painting as a whole:

The invention, taste, drawing, colour, touch, sentiment, all differ. One feels oneself transported into another world, far away, and unknown . . . An English picture is as modern as a novel by Balzac: the most advanced civilization is manifest in the tiniest details, in the brilliance of the varnish, in the preparation of the . . . colours. Everything is perfect.

It was then in British art that those qualities of spontaneity and directness, of fluency and swiftness, that came to animate the most advanced painters of the continent and to give birth to Impressionism, were chiefly to be found, and they were most pronounced in watercolour.

There was indeed nothing across the channel to compare with the achievements of the British watercolourists in boldness of conception, freedom of execution and frank celebration of the qualities inherent in the medium itself. One looks in vain for equivalents of J R Cozens or de Wint, Cotman or Turner. It is not true, as is often claimed, that watercolour was a British invention, nor even that it had always been used with the utmost skill in Britain; but it is certainly true that during the period when it reached its perfection here, it had fallen into decline in continental Europe, being used tentatively or not at all, and playing no part in the development of painting as a whole. In Britain, on the other hand, the more robust and painterly approach to oil painting, and the conception of subject matter itself, at least in landscape, had for years been very closely connected to advances made in watercolour. Some of the most important painters worked in both media, and Turner, by many standards the greatest of them all, achieved some of his most splendid triumphs in oil through the deliberate adaptation of techniques he had developed in his watercolours.

Watercolour is, of course, a medium uniquely adapted to convey spontaneous response and transient effect, to record shifting lights, mists and vapours; its fluidity and transparency are analogous to the elements of air or water. It is the perfect medium for landscape, and the growing appreciation of its special qualities changed the perception of landscape itself. Used on its own, and it took artists many years to learn to do this, it tends inescapably to abstraction of form and tone, and to its own self-definition. Watercolour is easily portable; a small box of colours and a sketchbook could, and frequently did, accompany an artist far afield. Thus equipped, and with his own eyes and feelings to guide him, he could leave behind not only the paraphernalia of the conventional studio, but much of the mental baggage that, at least in the eighteenth century, went with it. Again, watercolour is essentially a medium for private activity, and it was even

Albrecht Dürer, *Alpine Landscape* c 1494–5, brush drawing in watercolour and body colour, The Visitors of the Ashmolean Museum, Oxford (not in exhibition)

more so early in our period when it possessed no independent status as an art form, and did not rank in the established hierarchies of art. Even when a sense of professionalism and identity did begin to develop among watercolourists, and in the early years of the nineteenth century special exhibition facilities were provided for them, the medium remained as much the preserve of the amateur. In fact some of the most remarkable advances in its handling were made by them, and by the numerous drawing masters – often like Malchair little more than amateurs themselves – who taught them.

By its very nature, watercolour lent itself to imaginative development free from many considerations of convention and commerce. More than the easel painter whose eye was fixed on the exhibition, the watercolourist could engage in private communication with his materials and with his subject. It is no accident that many of the most audacious and

prophetic compositions to be found in our period emerged in watercolour, for in the history of art at least since the Renaissance, the medium has consistently produced works that stand outside their time. Travelling from Nuremberg to Venice on his first visit to Italy in 1494, Albrecht Dürer paused to make some extraordinary watercolours of Alpine valleys (above) whose clarity of vision, rhythmic balance of design and modulated tone astonishingly prefigure the achievements of Romantic watercolourists working directly from nature 300 years later. Even more prophetic, and of a time nearer our own, is the fact that Dürer apparently felt no need to 'finish' his drawings; minutely detailed passages and the merest suggestions happily co-exist in a harmony that seems to spring from something deeper than the artist's failure to devote any more time to the subject. Scarcely less remarkable in their way are the handful of lovely studies that the young Anthony Van Dyck

13

JONATHAN SKELTON
The Ponte Molle and the Tiber in Flood 1758

made of scenery around Rye in the 1630s – surely working outdoors, in an impromptu rapture as if overjoyed to cast aside for a moment the concerns of his portrait-painting career. Both Dürer and Van Dyck were magnificently 'off-duty' in these beautiful drawings. They were responding to the stimulus of travel to new places with fresh and unprejudiced eyes, and using their medium to fullest advantage.

Travel, as we shall see, was to be a consistently liberating force for generations of watercolourists, and it was largely in search of imaginative and technical liberation that the young Jonathan Skelton set off to Italy to study in 1757. He had received some training, but his main object in going abroad was to rid himself of his teacher's style and find one distinctly his own. Both this resolutely independent spirit, and his predilection for watercolour itself, were extremely unusual in their day. For water-colour had yet to achieve the status it would acquire

in the next thirty years, and when used by British artists, was usually treated merely as a local tint for drawings made chiefly in outline. The vast majority of such drawings were topographical in content, intended for engraving, so that monochrome washes were as often used as others. The sole purpose of such drawings was to convey information; artists had no need to ask themselves questions while making them. Yet Skelton was determined to escape from conventional disciplines, and to develop watercolour as a medium for response to pure landscape, wherever possible outdoors. It is true that he did not start out with this resolve; his earliest attempts in Italy were in open-air painting in oil. But having failed at this he decided to paint, as he quaintly put it, 'with a body in Water-Colours after Nature'. His Italian watercolours (above), the first significant group of drawings of Rome and its environs to be made by a British artist in the eighteenth century, certainly do

ALEXANDER COZENS
Landscape with Fir Trees

GÜNTHER BRUS
Untitled 1960

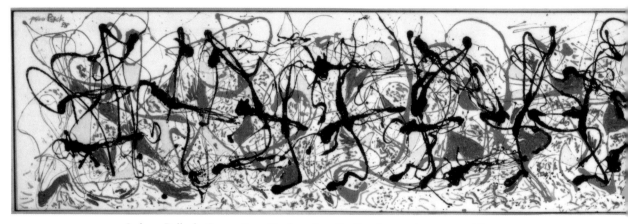

Jackson Pollock, *Summertime: Number 9A* 1948, oil and enamel on canvas, The
Trustees of the Tate Gallery (not in exhibition)

not escape the compositional conventions of classical
landscape; but to aspire to such pictorial effects in
watercolour was original in itself, and even more so
when combined with bright clear colour and vibrant
natural forms of trees and plants. Eight months into
his Roman stay he was delighted to report home the
comment of a fellow Englishman that 'he could not
tell what Master I imitated, He thought my Manner
like Nature's Manner'. Skelton had done what all the
artists in this exhibition did; he had struck out on his
own.

If Skelton was notable above all for his independence, for his retreat from a received style and
rejection of a master, Alexander Cozens turned his
position as a drawing master into a springboard for
far more radical inventions in technique and concept.
'As full of systems as the universe', in William
Beckford's description, he it was nevertheless who
elevated ideas of chance and accident into a system of
their own, and into the substance of art, by asserting
the primacy and independence of the medium itself.
In Cozens's hands, his materials became cause as well
as effect. Cozens's 'blot' method was an inspired
invention. Its chief motivation had been to provide
pupils who lacked skill in drawing with the possibi-
lity of creating a picture, but it had implications far
beyond this. The concept was simple enough; a
brush or pen was loaded with ink and flicked across a
page, and the resulting splashes, combined or linked,
were used as the basis for making landscape compositions of simple grandeur, built around abstract
forms of rocks, mountains and trees (p 15). The

ability to make such combinations depended on
received assumptions of what would make appropriate compositions, and these Cozens provided in his
book, *A New Method of Assisting the Invention in
Drawing Original Compositions of Landscape*, published with acquatint illustrations (p 4). His text
makes it clear that he did not intend the initial blot to
be wholly fortuitous, but rather an expression of a
'general idea' that would then be developed as the
blot was worked up. This, too, was consistent with
the conceptual approach announced in the introduc-
tion: 'Composing landscape by invention, is not the
act of imitating individual nature; it is more; it is
forming artificial representations of landscape on
general principles of nature, founded in unity of
character, which is true simplicity; concentrating in
each individual composition the beauties, which
judicious imitation would select from those which
are dispersed by nature'.

This is as traditional as it is progressive a view,
looking back to the formal grandeur of classical
landscape and forwards to abstraction. But while the
blot method was not an excuse for a totally random
approach, it did suggest a new acceptance of the
medium as a determinant, of at least a certain degree
of automatism in technique and of its relationship to
psychological states, that anticipates much that has
happened in our century. It is no accident that plates
in *A New Method* have a surreal quality, and the blot
method might almost be a blueprint for Günther
Brus in his large 'Untitled' of 1960 (p 15), where dark
colour swirls and coalesces on the paper and, without

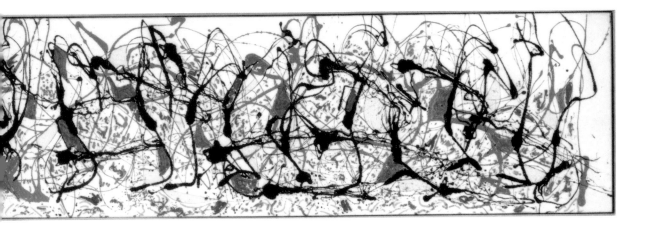

alluding to any particular object or element, acts powerfully on our imagination. Certainly Cozens stepped quite outside his time when he wrote: 'An artificial blot will suggest different ideas to different persons; on which account it has the strongest tendency to enlarge the powers of invention, be more effectual to that purpose than the study of nature alone'.

Cozens's originality was not confined to his liberated attitude to technique and an appreciation of the relationship between medium and mind. At a time when draughtsmen were mainly bound by outline, and paid little attention to tone, he realised that 'in nature forms are not distinguished by lines, but by shade and colour'. In that remark lay the promise of many of the finest achievements of English watercolour, but for Cozens himself monochrome washes, sombre greys, browns and ochre yellows were sufficient. His landscapes are landscapes of the mind, composed in broad and simple masses, and as often asymmetric as they are classically balanced. They are, essentially, abstract. They are also expressive. In Cozens's thought and art we may well detect the origins of a sensibility that looks forward both to the monumental simplicity of Mark Rothko's colour fields, and to the structured accidents of Jackson Pollock's drip paintings, in which rhythmic scatterings of paint combine to form a meditation on the grandeur and vastness of the American landscape (above).

By any standards Alexander Cozens is exceptional. The achievement of William Pars may at first seem less distinctive today, yet made at least as great an impression in its time. Pars was among the very first of those watercolourists of the mid-eighteenth century to find a profound inspiration in travel and to rise above the imitative disciplines of commissioned topography to new heights of feeling and technical skill. Aged twenty-two in 1764, he was hired by the Oxford antiquarian Richard Chandler to record the classical ruins of Greece and Asia Minor, sponsored by the Society of Dilettanti. Two years later he submitted to the Society a series of large views in which the cool analysis essential to such a project was modified by a subtle and sensitive handling of watercolour all the more remarkable in that his earliest training had been as a figure and portrait painter, and in the drawings for Chandler he was effectively teaching himself as he went along. Though largely free of individual mannerisms, Pars's style is always his own, invented like Skelton's for his own purpose, and his friend and fellow painter Thomas Jones rightly observed that he 'worked after nature, with a taste peculiar to himself'.

The drawings made for Chandler won Pars his most important patron, the 2nd Viscount Palmerston, a member of the Dilettanti, and it was with Palmerston that Pars made the journey to the Swiss Alps in 1770 that produced perhaps his finest and most expressive watercolours. Their colouring is clear and pure, their modelling always crisp, achieved through combinations of fine pen-work with a mesh of individual touches of the brush in related tones. There is a certain detachment in Pars's

WILLIAM PARS
On the Tessin near Poleggio

JOHN ROBERT COZENS
The Gulf of Salerno c 1790

JOHN ROBERT COZENS
The Entrance to the Valley of the Grande Chartreuse in Dauphiné
c 1783

vision, but far from depriving his drawings of atmosphere, this seems to have given him a particular affinity with wild and remote subjects such as glaciers or ice flows. The Swiss drawings show a tendency – developed further in his later work in Ireland and Italy – towards a more painterly approach to the medium. In the rather intimate study of a bridge over a waterfall shown here (p 18) the washes are deployed densely with a loaded brush, and mixed in places with gum arabic to achieve effects reminiscent of oil. Pars's patron was evidently especially pleased; 'Marvellous' was his verdict, in a note on the drawing's mount.

Travel to Switzerland and Italy was a common theme in the careers of a number of distinguished watercolourists. In 1776, a continental journey through Switzerland to Rome in the retinue of the young connoisseur Richard Payne Knight liberated the genius of Alexander Cozens's son John Robert, and initiated his development into one of the greatest and most original of all watercolourists. Cozens repeated the journey in 1782 with William Beckford. These continental tours formed the basis of his art; his drawings and sketches, made from nature and subsequently worked up, were later repeated in the form of large and finished watercolours. John Robert retained his father's broad and schematic approach, his poetic conception, and added a profoundly introspective melancholy of his own. Unlike his father's, his drawings were always rooted in topographical fact, but their breadth of handling, solemn and restricted palette and elimination of particulars can give them an almost lunar quality, or instil in the viewer a nostalgia for some other world of memory or myth. His vision was sometimes classical, as in the 'Gulf of Salerno' (p 18), and at others quirky and asymmetric. Paul Oppé's comment on one of Cozens's Italian drawings, that it was a 'composition that surpasses itself', could apply to most of Cozens's finest work.

A drawing of that remotest of Alpine passes, the Grande Chartreuse (p 19), conveys an infinity of space within a small compass. To capture the silence and bleakness of the Chartreuse, Cozens gives us a splendid abstraction, free of topographical detail and of pictorial convention. Deep washes of purple, blue and greyish green reverberate on the page, suggesting scale, mass and organic life. Broad sweeps of the

brush give way to delicate vertical touches to indicate the trees clinging to the inhospitable rock. Cozens's was a wholly intuitive approach, a world away from the context of descriptive topography that had originally justified such drawings. Cozens, said Constable, was 'all poetry', and his art, ranging in character from elegaic classicism to austere abstraction, was likewise a powerful influence on the young Turner.

The 'Grande Chartreuse' is timeless, and has as much in common with Rothko's resonant colour as with anything done in its own century. Much of Cozens's originality lay in the equivalences he discovered between mood and colour. His colours are not 'real', yet they seem to offer a memory of reality as definitive as it is subjective. All the eighteenth century traveller's loneliness and apprehension in the Alps, all the grand tourists's yearning and nostalgia for the Italy of his youth, is comprehended in his drawings. Like his father's, his was an art of tone, not line. Observing the workings of his splendidly liberated brush, and recognising his predisposition to generalise and economise in his rendering of mass, it is tempting to disparage a more linear approach and to relegate the tinted outline drawing henceforth to a backwater. Yet originality lies not in method alone, but in the way an artist interprets it. Looking ahead, we are bound to applaud the economy and vigour of outline in the neo-classical drawings of Blake and John Flaxman as innovatory, and in Cozens's time another artist, Francis Towne, had demonstrated that the tinted outline could itself be transformed into a style of extraordinary lucidity, and one, moreover, with its own imperatives towards a kind of abstraction.

Towne had shared some training in London with Pars, who remained a lifelong friend, and he later joined that group of drawing masters whose contemporary reputations were fleeting or local, if they existed at all, but whose work has since been gathered into a noble pantheon. His career had begun promisingly enough, as an oil painter, and it was only in 1777, when he made a tour of Wales, that he began to work regularly in watercolours and to develop the unique style that reached its peak in 1780–81 when he travelled to Italy and Switzerland. The basis of Towne's drawing was a taut and sharp pen outline, reduced to a rigorous simplicity to

FRANCIS TOWNE
The Bay of Naples c 1781

express only the essential structure of a scene, over which bright colour was laid in flat planes. He possessed an unerring sense of pattern and design; his eye was as reductive as Cozens's though his technical means were very different. Like Cozens again, he was not afraid to break pictorial rules, choosing odd or irregular angles of vision, subverting conventional perspective or correct scale, and ruthlessly eliminating details he considered extraneous. In a drawing of the Bay of Naples (above) he attained an extreme of minimalism hardly found outside Oriental drawing with a few vertical and horizontal strokes of the pen and a float of the palest monochrome wash. On other occasions he worked with brilliant, jewel colours, sometimes mixed with gum arabic to enrich them, laid over fine thickly woven paper.

Whenever he could, Towne drew 'on the spot', and emphasised his outdoor activity in annotations to his drawings. Open air nature study has, of course, a particular resonance for the historian, for it forms part of the wider story that leads to Impressionism and to much else besides. Certainly it has been when working outdoors – in whatever media – that artists have managed to transcend contemporary conventions, and indeed often their own artistic style. Nowhere is this more true than in the case of the marine painter Nicholas Pocock, if only because his finished watercolours of landscapes and marines are so dully methodical. Pocock had been advised to work outdoors in colours by Joshua Reynolds, who passed on advice he had received in Rome from the French painter Claude-Joseph Vernet, whose outdoor sketches had struck Reynolds 'for that truth which those works only have which are produced while the impression is warm from Nature'. The results of this encouragement can be seen in a couple of exquisite on-the-spot studies, spread across the pages of a sketchbook, of Pistyll Ghaedra in North Wales (p 22). Pocock has engaged closely with his subject. Instead of Towne's almost sculptural linearity he has achieved an atmospheric and vaporous effect, anticipating Turner and the Romantics in his subtle interpretation of the prismatic sparkle of the cascade – an effect emphasised by his having written the word 'Steam' across its spray. For a brief moment, this rather staid artist has reached a new height of empirical naturalism, and revealed a fresh

NICHOLAS POCOCK
Waterfall: Pistyll Ghaedra

concern for fleeting phenomena as well as more solid matter like trees and rocks. No less striking a dichotomy between an inspired private response to nature and a conventional public performance occurs with the pastel portraitist John Downman, who at Albano, on an Italian tour in 1744–5, made some very remarkable large watercolour studies of trees and plants. Like Towne, Downman has chosen what interests him and eliminated the rest. He has adopted a low viewpoint, almost as if lying on the ground, so as to involve himself in the organic life of plants and roots. His subtle tinting with pale colours is there to suggest the play of light rather than to match local tints literally (right).

An artist's response to nature is a sure test of his originality. By the later eighteenth century, a host of drawing masters could provide guidelines for dealing with trees, rocks or water, but the interesting artists are those who first provided them, or discovered a way of their own. Downman, selecting a single tree and its satellite plants, responded with a drawing that combined calligraphic outline with atmospheric tinting. Peter de Wint, decades later, preferred to draw loosely with a wet and laden brush and a limited palette – most effectively in the private landscape studies he referred to for his exhibition pieces. The poet John Clare famously described his most characteristic watercolours as 'rough sketches, taken in the fields, that breathe the living freshness of open air and sunshine, where the harmony of earth, air and sky form such a happy union of greens and greys'. At Lowther in the late 1830s de Wint made a study of trees growing from a bank that shows his selective eye and bold touch at their very best (right). Eschewing detail he concentrated on pattern and light; the opposing diagonals of trees and grassy slope create a powerful geometry, and areas of blank paper convey the splash of sunlight falling through the branches. De Wint's was an enquiry into what he perceived as the essential structure of landscape as rigorous as anything attempted by Cézanne (right). Likewise, John Sell Cotman's limpid study of trees at Brandsby (right) addresses the rhythms and patterns of natural growth, and enveloping light, in simple terms and pellucid washes. He too displayed an unerring sense of design as he set down the essentials of the scene, following his own advice to his son: 'Draw sternly and true, *Leave out, but add nothing*'.

JOHN DOWNMAN
Tree Trunk near Albano 1774

PETER DE WINT
Study of Trees at Lowther c 1839

Paul Cezanne, *The Avenue at the Jas de Bouffon* c 1874–5, oil on canvas,
The Trustees of the Tate Gallery (not in exhibition)

JOHN SELL COTMAN
Near Brandsby, Yorkshire 1805

CORNELIUS VARLEY
Evening at Llanberis 1805

MARK ROTHKO
Untitled (Brown and Grey) 1968–9

Drawings like these may well be seen as tending towards the abstract, and such an inclination is particularly to be found in the nature studies of the Romantics. Moreover, their curiosity about the natural world led them to places and positions that were not traditional in art (unless they were imagined). In purely aesthetic terms, the results of their studies contained the potential for a new pictorial language. The mountain studies of the brothers John and Cornelius Varley, for example, are both precise and objective in purpose and abstract in effect. To look down on the world from a great height was, if not a new experience, at least one quite new to art. Wordsworth, in that rather unsatisfactory poem *Peter Bell*, imagined his hero flying over the Alps, and surveying them beneath him 'like waters in commotion'. The image was a telling one partly because of the imaginative leap required to place oneself in such a position, and partly because of its comparison of one manifestation of nature with another. John Varley, looking down upon the lake of Bala from Cader Idris at sunrise in 1804, saw the rounded peaks of the lesser slopes below him almost as an ocean swell; his drawing is extraordinary for its utter simplicity and emptiness, and visionary in its intensity, like Caspar David Friedrich's paintings of high mountains. Alas, John Varley's public art was a very different matter, reflecting his remark that 'Nature wants cooking'. Cornelius was more consistent in his search for simple truths. Concentrating on a ridge at Llanberis one evening in 1805 he responded with broad bands of colour flooded across a soaked sheet to create the simplest tonal match (p 24). Doubtless he intended no more than a private record of a luminous climatic effect, but to the modern eye his little watercolour has all the mysterious grandeur and feeling of a Rothko colour field in miniature (p 25). From the position Cornelius reached here, total abstraction seems but a blink away.

Yet there was another way to look at mountains. For John Ruskin, an impression determined by light, the sort we might achieve by looking at a subject through half-closed eyes, or a single sighting such as might be obtained in a photograph, was not enough. Rather it was vital to penetrate to the underlying structure of the mass. To draw a mountain required both precise geological knowledge and an empathy with the dynamic forces of nature; an artist's business

was 'not so much what the forms of the earth actually are, as what they are continually becoming'. Ruskin drew not to record impressions, nor to make views, but as part of a system of research, and he came more and more to reject current pictorial values in favour of concentration on the details that he considered intrinsically important. The essential organic structure of the motif in question, whether mountain, tree, rock or flower, must determine the way in which it is drawn; the artist 'must adopt the order in description, which Nature seems to have adopted in formation'. In the case of a cluster of trees outside Bologna that he saw in 1847 or 1848, this meant a leaping, flame-like pen line (right), and in that of the Aiguilles of Chamouni, a tough, tense line in pencil with strong, rhythmic accents to express the system of harmonious curves formed by cleavage in the rock. It would, he wrote of his magnificent drawing of the Aiguille Blaitière from the Montanvert (right), be easy to miss this essential feature:

> . . . an ordinary artist would draw rather the cragginess and granulation of the surfaces, but . . . as an artist increases in acuteness of perception, the facts which become outward and apparent to him are those which bear upon the make and growth of the thing . . . [The] keenness of the artist's eye may almost precisely be tested by the degree in which he perceives the curves that give [the aiguilles] their strength and grace, and in harmony with which the flakes of granite are bound together, like the bones and jaw of a saurian.

Stressing the scientific legitimacy of his drawing, Ruskin annotated it as 'showing finest conchoidal – riband structure J R on the spot, 1849'. Ruskin represented a wholly new attitude to the inner morality of landscape and to the function and appearance of art. In his view, beauty was no substitute for understanding. Yet while he emphasised the accuracy and clarity of his studies of rocks or plants with burning passion, he also felt an empathy and emotional involvement with the natural world that sprang from his own imagination. Nature seemed to him a model for a moral and ethical order, but as the years went by, that order revealed itself to him as random, illogical, even cruel in its constant metamorphosis. Ruskin's characteristic comparison

JOHN RUSKIN
View of Bologna 1845 or 1846

JOHN RUSKIN
Aiguille Blaitière 1849

of form with form in his notes to his drawing of Chamouni – the curves of the aiguille to the grain of wood or 'the bones and jaw of a saurian' – shows him endeavouring to make an all-embracing sense of the parts he studied so assiduously in detail, but his apprehension of what things were 'continually becoming', subjective as it was, was impossible to reconcile with scientific objectivity. More recent artists have been perhaps more honest in acknowledging the primacy of their imaginative response, as when Günther Brus and Arnolf Rainer evolved a sinister mask-like form from some botanical motifs of Ruskinian precision in the sinister 'No, Daphne, No!' of 1984 (p 30), or Wols deployed composite biomorphic shapes with an ambiguity as deliberate as it is suggestive in his untitled painting of 1944–5 (illustrated on the back cover). Such images are far closer to Ruskin's emotional response to nature than might at first be imagined.

Ruskin's hero and mentor was Turner, but his teacher, in 1834, had been A V Copley Fielding, the President of the Society of Painters in Water-Colours, who had himself been taught by John Varley. Since the foundation of the first watercolour society in 1805, its exhibitions had given watercolour a new status as a public art, and artists had vied with each other to produce ever grander subjects and to confirm the medium's transition from 'drawing' to 'painting'. Fielding's 'Cader Idris' (p 32) may strike us as a conventional example of the view made for exhibition – certainly if compared with his master's observations from the summit of the same mountain or with his pupil's geological investigations. Yet it embodies qualities of luminosity, and spatial breadth emphasised by an extraordinarily wide angle of vision and shallow height, that might almost remind us of Pollock's confrontation with 'the vast horizontality of the land' in his 'Summertime', that were not at all to be taken for granted at the time. Ruskin, though he later criticised Fielding's manner as facile, paid tribute to his 'faithful and simple rendering of nature'; he admired his mastery of hazy atmosphere and far horizons, and movingly praised him for 'casting his whole soul into space'. It might seem that Fielding had little of fundamental value to teach such a pupil as Ruskin; his imagination was entirely pictorial, and harnessed to the production of popular exhibition pieces. Yet Ruskin's search for the underlying structural order of the natural world may partly be traced if not to Fielding himself, at least to his brother Thales, whose book *On the Theory of Painting* expressed the function of the imitative artist as the discovery of 'the reasoning power in the formation of things'. Through the intelligent act of drawing, the artist could perceive essential truths.

Fielding's mastery of the extended picture space owed something to John Varley, but most to the example of Thomas Girtin, together with Turner the most remarkable and innovatory of all the Romantic watercolourists. Girtin had studied with Turner as a youth in the evening 'Academy' of the amateur and collector, Dr Thomas Monro, who showed them besides much else the works of J R Cozens; and these, together with the doctor's conceptual approach to his own drawings of picturesque scenery – he called them his 'imaginings' – helped spur them to transform the topographical through looser handling and luminous and atmospheric effects. In each case, the result was to be an inspired mastery of pure watercolour, a triumphant realisation of the powers inherent in the medium itself.

Girtin and Turner are so often compared that it is easy to miss the great difference between their approaches, when in fact an appreciation of these can only stress the originality of each. Whereas Turner achieved many of his most spectacular effects by spangled veils of local tints over broad foundations, Girtin remained wedded to the broad tonal approach of Cozens, but carried it to new heights of expression and subtle delicacy. His mature work, from the last couple of years of his tragically short life, matches breadth of handling with breadth of vision in a perfect balance that consistently surprises and delights; it has an internal logic of colour and form that, having once struck us, seems inevitable. Among Girtin's most expansive and atmospheric compositions, and a display of his materials used with a deceptive simplicity, is the 'White House at Chelsea', of 1800 (right). It is a vision of almost Whistlerian refinement and economy: a mood of transcendental calm rises from the glassy waters of the Thames, spread before us on a parallel plane to emphasise the extent of the river; trees and buildings are silhouetted on a low horizon, as in a Rembrandt etching, and the white house – in truth just a blank patch in the off-white paper – locks the whole composition together.

THOMAS GIRTIN
The White House at Chelsea 1800

GÜNTHER BRUS and ARNULF RAINER
No, Daphne, No! 1984

PETER DE WINT
Cliveden on Thames c 1812

EDWARD LEAR
Substructure of the Palace of Septimus Severus, Palatine c 1838

While very young, Girtin had learned how to adjust space and perspective for dramatic effect. Here he further romanticised the subject by a sunset light.

Girtin's expanses of space, broad handling and restrained tonality affected British watercolour long after his premature death in 1802. He had no more resolute admirer than Peter de Wint, who, apart from Turner, was one of the three or four dominant watercolourists of the 1820s and 1830s. De Wint's work is often a tribute to Girtin in its wide horizontality and subdued colour, yet the manner is distinctive – freer, laid in with generous sweeps of a damper brush as in his view of Cliveden on Thames (left). In his extraordinary 'Westmorland Hills, bordering the Ken' (p 33), de Wint took the wide panorama to its furthest extreme, challenging traditional notions of picture-making in favour of an angle of vision that is in fact closer to natural vision, and, by the inevitable omission of distracting foreground details, affords immediate access to the subject; indeed de Wint has drawn the eye into the picture space still more urgently by creating inward thrusts of cart-track and curving hay-stooks.

Edward Lear, working towards a study of the Palace of Septimus Severus in Rome, probably in 1838 (above), can also be seen widening and lowering his view, laying it out parallel with the picture plane in a Girtinesque manner and building it up with broad and economical washes of flat colour. But Lear's composition is structured very differently from de Wint's. His horizontals are becoming a negation of depth. The straight stretch of wall across the foreground, which he has not finished, closes off the middle distance, just as the palace does the far distance. Lear's drawing is an arrangement of self-contained planes, and if Fielding and de Wint had opened up an infinity of space, Lear, at least on this occasion, seems to be experimenting with a certain flatness.

The history of modern art has sometimes been written in terms of a 'road to flatness' along which such experiments as the abandonment of conventional perspective, the closing off or restriction of background and distance, and the creation of deliberately perverse or illogical spaces, were stages leading to the complete absence of space, to the construction of pure colour or shape on the flat plane of the working surface as, for example, Picasso did

ANTHONY VANDYKE COPLEY FIELDING
Cader Idris from the Barmouth Sands 1810

by means of collage in his café still life of 1913 (p 34), or Brice Marden in purely abstract terms in his 'I' (p 35). There is a tendency to equate the absence of space in works like Marden's with absence of meaning or rationale. In fact 'I' is specifically about the classical tradition, and as much a tribute to it as Lear's view of ancient Rome. It expresses classical ideals of symmetry and logic through an architectonic arrangement of planes of colour, bounded by a clear outline. There is nothing really new in this. Flat colour, and space-denying composition, can be found as active agents of pictorial structure and meaning in earlier artists too – and above all in watercolour which of all mediums is best able to produce smooth and unmodulated surfaces.

For John Flaxman, a certain flatness of design and handling and a restricted palette seemed, as it evidently did for Marden, contiguous with the idea of classicism. As a neo-classical sculptor, he took a wide sheet of paper as the starting point for a frieze-like relief design of a processional subject in which, as in a Roman sarcophagus carving, background space is almost entirely denied (p 35). For the landscapists, flat colour planes did not imply absence of space or depth; far from it. Towne, who relished vast and empty subjects and often chose unpredictable viewpoints to enhance their power, used flat washes in conjunction with a searching linear structure as a means of reducing forms to their essentials. This concentration on basic facts, this use of colour planes as building blocks to define the essence of a subject, which was to be the central task of Cézanne and the

Cubists, appears also in the most personal watercolours of Joshua Cristall, such as his 'Beach Scene at Hastings' shown here (p 34), and in William Henry Brooke's splendidly economical analysis of a road and cliff at Lanherne Bay (p 36). For John Sell Cotman it was the absolute cornerstone of his art.

Cotman's finest watercolours are constructions of flat washes in bright and unmodulated tones, beautifully harmonised and organised with a refined sense of pattern. His study of trees at Brandsby (p 23) is a product of the last of three visits to Yorkshire, in 1805, that brought his genius to full maturity and released a vein of intensely lyrical naturalism. Its originality lies not in the pastoral subject, but in what the scholar and collector Sidney Kitson described as the 'translation of an ordinary scene into a patterned harmony at the hands of an inspired artist'. His characteristic construction of his composition by masses of plain wash, laid light against dark, is already evident here, while in the interior of Norwich cathedral drawn three years later (p 37), this method is even more boldly exploited, for a subject that is in itself original in interpretation. The interior of a great Gothic cathedral was a thoroughly conventional theme, usually treated either with awed respect for soaring facades or shadowy vaulting, or with the learned zeal of the antiquarian. Cotman, on the other hand, has chosen an unpromising corner and a difficult angle, and has cropped the image so that it has the haphazard feel of a Parisian street painted by an Impressionist; the curve of the ambulatory is sharply interrupted, as in an interior

PETER DE WINT
Westmorland Hills, bordering the Ken c 1830–35

by Matisse, by an arched screen. Yet these eccentricities are legitimised – indeed transfigured – by Cotman's tautness of design, boldness of colour and emphatic light and shade. Cotman at his best still seems extraordinarily modern in sensibility and technique. Neither his analytical style nor his personal approach to subject matter was appreciated in his own day, and his patron Francis Cholmeley, thinking to do him a service, passed on the advice that 'two-thirds of mankind, you know, mind more about *what* is represented than *how* it is done'.

Cotman's achievement is consistent, and he is generally unmistakable. Turner, whose epic career as a watercolourist was only part of his wider achievement, was infinitely varied and always inventive in both 'what' and 'how' he represented. He is the greatest of all Romantic watercolourists, and has been left almost to the last for he forms the measure of almost all the artists working in the medium in the first half of the nineteenth century. He was the acknowledged leader of a group who transformed the art of view-making by their sense of appropriate detail, spatial amplitude and atmospheric effect; by a new naturalism and by overt acknowledgement of their own emotional response.

Turner was of course an oil painter as well as a watercolourist, and his achievements in both areas were inter-dependent, for his early watercolours aspired to the power of oil – and indeed the history of art shows few more daring voyages of discovery into the latent possibilities of a medium – while his later oils assumed a translucency of colour and a repertoire

of peculiarly effective mannerisms, from delicate and refined layers of brilliant local colour to scrabblings with brush handle or finger nail, that he had developed as a draughtsman. In its consistent complexity, his use of watercolour was from early on the opposite of Girtin's or Cotman's. Even his youthful search for breadth and grandeur was impelled by a more urgent and restless vision of the 'Sublime' than Girtin's and indeed Turner re-invented the notion, as he did so much else, not least by an impulse to engage in the realities of the magnificent scenery that he pursued so assiduously at home and abroad, and by the naturalism that resulted from it. His magnificent 'Traeth Mawr' (p 38), with its bold, bright colours loosely applied, perhaps in the open air before the motif, is one of a group of large, experimental colour studies made in North Wales in 1798 and 1799 that marked a new departure in his work and a new realisation of the painterly power of watercolour. It is a full-blooded essay in the mountainous 'Sublime' and in some ways shows Turner rather close to Girtin, but its colour has an outdoor freshness and Turner's handling of the brush is already thoroughly liberated. Moreover Turner's sense of scale was grander than Girtin's. In sheer size his work was outstanding, and in this sense perhaps anticipates the impulse of largeness and monumentality that has characterised much modern painting. In the vastness of their canvases and the dynamism of their handling, the Abstract Expressionists may be said to have rediscovered something of the new sense of the 'Sublime' that animated the young Turner when he

33

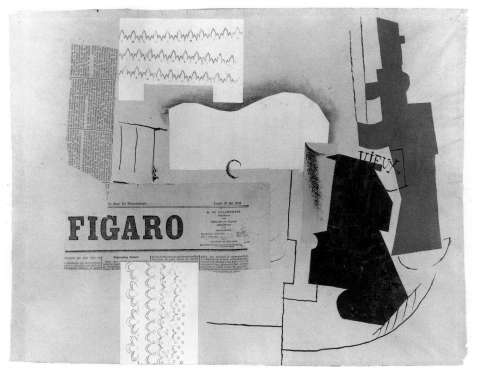

PABLO PICASSO
Bottle of Vieux Marc, Glass, Guitar and Newspaper 1913

JOSHUA CRISTALL
Beach Scene at Hastings c 1808

BRICE MARDEN
I 1986

JOHN FLAXMAN
Procession of Ancient British Priests c 1793

35

WILLIAM HENRY BROOKE
Lanherne Bay near the Nunnery, Cornwall 1819

JOHN SELL COTMAN
Interior of the Eastern Ambulatory of the Apse, Norwich Cathedral
1808

J M W TURNER
Traeth Mawr, with Y Cnicht and Moelwyn Mawr? 1799

J M W TURNER
A Ravine on the Pass of St. Gothard 1802

J M W TURNER
Castel dell'Ovo, Naples, Capri and Sorrento in the Distance 1819

adapted the pictorial language of his time to the mountains of Wales.

From such noble panoramas Turner moved to a much closer experience of the 'Sublime', in the Alps in 1802. His drawings from that year anticipate Ruskin's concern with the structure of natural things, and create a record of organic mass and growth that seems to evoke a sense of the wider order and harmony of life. Turner's cleft of rock in a ravine on the St Gothard Pass (left) seems almost a sexual metaphor, and indeed his relationship with his natural subject matter was a profoundly physical one. Like Richard Long today he climbed it, walked it, was soaked and blown and warmed by it; and no painter has insisted more than Turner on the actuality of these experiences, even if, unlike the Impressionists who looked to his example, he increasingly came to paint from recollection rather than in the field.

Turner's watercolours were in fact rarely made outdoors, although his sparkling sketch of Benson, done in 1805, almost certainly was (p 41). By now Turner was using his medium with complete spontaneity, dappling limpid washes over the page of a sketchbook, leaving plenty of paper bare to mark highlights of sunshine flickering across meadows on a breezy summer day. As always, the approach is dynamic and intuitive, adapted to the purpose in hand and careless of received method. While he was still young, Joseph Farington had observed that 'Turner has no settled method but drives the colours about till he has expressed the idea in his mind'. Yet Turner always displayed a natural gift for picture making. Although Ruskin looked to him as the inspiration of his own passionate inquiry into the structure of nature, Turner hardly ever scrutinised particular motifs. He did not make what he once described as 'pictures of bits', but rather organised them into a satisfying whole. His compositional structures were original and highly personal, even when they seem at first glance to conform to established prototypes. The view of Benson, which seems so simple and uncontrived, in fact displays one of his characteristic designs, a double perspective established by avenues of approach into the pictorial space, out from rather than converging at the centre: a track leads the eye away to the right, while the river and meadows also

WILLIAM JAMES MÜLLER
The Avon, 4 1834

invite it into the centre and the left distance; foreground detail is omitted altogether.

Turner, like Girtin, Fielding and De Wint, was a master of the extended picture space. His use of space was dynamic and active, as may be seen in the great panoramic sweep of the Bay of Naples beyond the Castel dell'Ovo in a watercolour made in 1819 (p 39), and with his genius for accumulating appropriate details and associations to establish sense of place, it was the essential factor in the creation of what Ruskin called 'Turnerian topography'. Utterly different from the painstaking description of the eighteenth century topographers, this was an art of exceptional richness and completeness, going beyond representative accuracy to attain an encyclopaedic image. Turner was as able to achieve this on a small scale as on a large; indeed some of the most remarkable displays of his unique approach to topography are to be seen in his designs for vignette illustrations, with their *multum in parvo* compression of riches into a tiny space.

The impact of these views without edges, the impression made by their own pictorial logic, can be seen in the splendidly simple and pared-down view of the Avon made by the Bristol artist W J Müller in 1834 (above), although Müller's approach here is otherwise the very opposite of Turner's in that he has left out the wealth of associative detail that Turner would have added, and has concentrated instead on simple masses and chiaroscuro. Müller has used his chosen format for an exercise in abstraction, and it is interesting to compare his view of a rocky and craggy subject with one of the more dramatic scenery of Ronda, drawn in exacting detail by David Roberts the same year, after a visit to Spain in 1823–4 (p 43). Like Turner, Roberts worked much for the engraver, and his drawing is highly wrought to convey a wealth of information and the particular feel of the place, which could then be approached only by a vertiginous track guarded by the Moorish castle in the foreground. Where Müller has generalised, Roberts has specified, marking the form and texture of the rock on which Ronda is built – not in Ruskin's strict geological way, but nevertheless with a sharpness and clarity that Ruskin admired. It was indeed the volume of lithographs of Roberts's *Picturesque Sketches in Spain* (1837) that first encouraged Ruskin to a 'more rich . . . true manner of

J M W TURNER
Benson (or Bensington), near Wallingford c 1805–6

WILLIAM CALLOW
Richmond Castle, Yorkshire 1843

delineation' – by which he meant a closer attention to detail and linear tension – and aroused the stirrings of the sensibility that enabled him so sensitively to appreciate Turner.

Roberts's approach to the pencil sketches in which he gathered the information he used for his watercolours was in fact very close to Turner's, elegant and concise, as it could only be if supported by a strong pictorial sense and a reliable visual memory. His friend and biographer James Ballantine remembered his 'faculty of photographing objects on his eye . . . he took in a large mass at one glance, not requiring to look again at that portion until he had completed it in his sketch. Other artists caught only small bits at a time and required to be renewing their glances continually'.

Travel remained for the late Romantics and Victorians, as it had been in the eighteenth century, a vital inspiration to the watercolourists. The vogue for books and annuals illustrated with continental views, the growing market for middle class travel in the years after the Napoleonic War, and the scope afforded by the popular watercolour exhibitions for large exhibition pieces, united to motivate artists to rove through Europe in search of subjects and to seek more vivid and dynamic patterns of composition and a more painterly technique. Views were now increasingly perceived as pictures, rather than as the personal and subjective record that they had often been, both for artists and their patrons, in the previous century. Artists like William Callow, shown here in a view of a picturesque subject at home (above), and James Holland, whose unfinished drawing of a canal at Rotterdam (p 44) is taken from a low angle that emphasises the soaring diagonal of a lock gate to create an image that is more than the sum of its parts – and one that might well qualify Degas's remark that no-one before his generation had drawn monuments from below – exemplify the more pictorial approach to watercolour.

These artists tended to use their washes with the clear, diluted, airy touch that had been particularly developed in the 1820s by Richard Parkes Bonington. In their work, and in that of the mature Turner, watercolour as a medium of transparency and translucency, perfectly equipped to convey light and atmosphere, may be said to reach its apogee. Yet at the same time, artists were advancing the medium

DAVID ROBERTS
Ronda, Spain 1834

JAMES HOLLAND
Rotterdam 1845

J M W TURNER
Rouen, the West Front of the Cathedral c 1832

J M W TURNER
Funeral at Lausanne 1841

in a quite different direction, making technique as well as composition a driving force for their pictorial aspirations. Combined with bodycolour, which today we know as gouache, watercolour drawings could take on a density and brilliance hardly imagined before; or, if darker ingredients like gum arabic were mixed with the washes, they could assume a sombre grandeur associated only with oil painting. Wherever our own preferences may lie – and modern taste has most often inclined to the more sensitive and delicate feeling of the translucent methods – we cannot but applaud the questioning attitude, the willingness to reinvent what would by the second quarter of the nineteenth century have seemed a thoroughly established tradition, that underpinned these more ambitious technical developments.

Both the subtlest transparency and the most intense brilliance and solidity of colour are to be found in Turner. His 'Funeral at Lausanne' is a triumph of limpid and diaphanous washes studded with delicate points of emphasis (above); by mixing his washes with bodycolour and using the finest tipped brushes he achieved the jewel-like glitter and profuse detail he favoured in the 1830s for drawings for engraving like that of Rouen Cathedral (p 45); and bodycolour, thrown boldly on a dark-toned paper, created the impressionistic drama of some entirely personal drawings of Venice made in 1833. While the magnificent chiaroscuro of his extra-ordinary drawing of a theatre at night (illustrated on the front cover) may be said to derive from Rembrandt, to whose spell Turner succumbed very enthusiastically in this decade, it remains an example of his unique ability to match method to subject and mood; it is absolutely modern in its vibrancy and expressive power.

Something of the same intuition and adaptability, combined with sensitivity to inspirations from earlier art, and the same search for rich and synoptic

SAMUEL PALMER
Villa d'Este, Tivoli c 1838

DAVID COX
Tour d'Horloge, Rouen 1829

effects, is to be found in Samuel Palmer. By the mid 1830s he had outgrown the wilful and archaising romanticism of his Shoreham period, when he had withdrawn from the world with all the yearning for a primitive innocence of feeling and expression that Gauguin felt in Tahiti, and was to be found adapting to the contemporary climate but still with a distinctive, personal touch. As with Turner, his finest work seems to grow visibly out of the physical act of drawing; he does not conceal the process, and his

drawings often appear unfinished. Lack of finish and technical refinement is sometimes commented upon adversely in the work of artists today, but Palmer makes it a positive virtue. In his magnificent 'Villa d'Este at Tivoli', of 1834 (p 47), passages of great elaboration are juxtaposed with areas where the pencil drawing seems still in a state of frenzied and unfocussed experimentation; perhaps Palmer was reminded (as Turner may have been of Rembrandt while watching the nocturnal illuminations of the

DAVID COX
Stone Bridge, Wales c 1850s

Venetian theatre) of the 'loose hatching and improvisamento' of ancient frescoes he had seen at Pompeii, in which 'joints and articulations are shaken out of the pencil'. Palmer has allowed the nervous, excited quality of his response to Tivoli, where 'Distances swarm everywhere but here are the finest trees and foregrounds combined with them', to become manifest in his technique. So too has David Cox in his drawing of the Tour d'Horloge at Rouen (left), perhaps the most inspired of a splendid group of studies he made on the continent in 1829. With its soaring vertical thrust and strongly marked effect of sunlight and shadow – effects typical of the dramatising pictorial tendencies of view painting in watercolour at this period – it would be impressive enough, but the bravura pencilling is no less striking.

Cox's drawings may seem at first the antithesis of the advice that Cox's fellow drawing master W H Pyne gave to his students, to 'substitute correctness of drawing for incoherancy and scrawling', but in fact not a mark is wasted. Cox's subject is a characteristic essay in the continental picturesque, a study of quaint and archaic architecture typical of its period; it is his technique that is distinctive. A feeling for the rustic 'Picturesque' of the late eighteenth century and also for the 'Sublime' matter of mountains and open spaces, also informed his work. He claimed that all that was required to form the Romantic vision was to be found in Wales, and it was there that he made the bold and direct drawing of a stone bridge (above) that shows his powerful late manner at its most rigorous and concentrated, and a new imaginative response that could find such a subject as legitimate and rewarding as a more conventional and predictable mountain panorama. The drawing has a tautness and energy in its attention to detail that might almost be compared to Ruskin's close-up geological studies, but even so, the image is perhaps essentially a 'Picturesque' one and does not represent the mature Cox at his most truly original.

It was in his large and grand exhibition watercolours on abstract themes, rendered with a bold and wonderfully loose brushwork, that Cox made the contribution that seems most modern today. Like Turner's last watercolours, 'The Night Train' (p 51) is both a summation of and a departure from all that had gone before, a fresh realisation of the watercolour medium in both technical and conceptual 49 terms. In a powerful vision of a train speeding across a flat, moonlit landscape, elemental forces created with a strong and spontaneous touch contend with the man-made power of steam. Cox contrasts man and nature, and past and present as represented by horse and rail, with all the poignancy and dramatic effect of Turner's 'Rain, Steam and Speed'. 'The Night Train' is a totally modern image, pregnant with the energy and also the uneasy apprehensions of a new age.

In 1850, perhaps a year after Cox painted 'The Night Train', John Frederick Lewis exhibited an exotic Egyptian Interior, 'The Hareem', at the Old Watercolour Society. It was a scrupulously detailed account of a scene as ancient and unchanging as Cox's was contemporary, and it represented the opposite of the broad, sweeping handling and tonal construction of Cox's drawing, but it too was considered a triumph of modernity. It was indeed a masterpiece of the latest watercolour style, rich and strong in colour, minute in detail, that seemed as revolutionary as the Pre-Raphaelitism that had now emerged in painting. Lewis's dramatic composition and feeling for glowing colour, achieved by the newly fashionable admixture of watercolour and bodycolour, had already appeared in the drawings he had made in Spain in 1832–4. There he had witnessed that momentous proclamation of Don Carlos that led to the Carlist Wars that ravaged Spain until 1876, and planned a picture of it that, had it progressed beyond the several superb studies he made for it (p 52), would have marked an epoch in modern history painting in watercolour.

These marvellous watercolours by Cox and Lewis could hardly be more different, yet represent wholly new understandings of the possibilities of their medium. They may seem a world away from the more tentative experiments of Jonathan Skelton with which we began. Yet neither Cox nor Lewis could have achieved what they did without benefitting from the questioning of methods and pictorial values, the continuing impulse to reinvent, the quest for a fresh and dynamic vision that would match the potential inherent in watercolour itself, so consistently pursued by its British practitioners during the past century.

Even if originality were judged to consist in newness or unfamiliarity of subject matter alone, Cox and Lewis would have amply met the criteria, the one by the contemporaneity, the other by the strangeness of his theme. But it is not in their subjects themselves, but in their interpretations of them, in their technical and compositional experiments, in their rigorous analysis of form and structure or the inspired confidence of their simplifications, that our 'original eyes' justify their presence here. Although this exhibition contains a predominance of landscapes, it is not about landscape, but about ways of seeing and painting that, during the period in question, were expressed most powerfully in response to the natural world. To paraphrase Alexander Cozens, these artists may have widely engaged in 'the study of nature alone', but they also 'enlarged the powers of invention', in ways that strike important chords today.

DAVID COX
Night Train c 1849

JOHN FREDERICK LEWIS
Study for 'The Proclamation of Don Carlos' c 1835–40

WORKS IN THE EXHIBITION

Dates are given when known.

Dimensions: height followed by width in millimetres.

Identification numbers are those of the Tate Gallery catalogue.

Page numbers refer to illustrations of the works.

WILLIAM HENRY BROOKE (1772–1860)
Lanherne Bay near the Nunnery, Cornwall 1819
Watercolour on paper
146 × 190
T03300 (p 36)

WILLIAM CALLOW (1812–1908)
Richmond Castle, Yorkshire 1843
Pen and watercolour on paper
337 × 514
N02435 (p 42)

JOHN CONSTABLE (1776–1837)
Cloud Study with Verses from [Robert] Bloomfield
c 1830s
Ink on paper
337 × 213
T01940 (p 11)

JOHN SELL COTMAN (1782–1842)
Near Brandsby, Yorkshire 1805
Pencil and watercolour on paper
329 × 228
The Visitors of the Ashmolean Museum, Oxford
(p 23)

JOHN SELL COTMAN (1782–1842)
Interior of the Eastern Ambulatory of the Apse,
Norwich Cathedral 1808
Pencil and watercolour on paper
395 × 272
The Visitors of the Ashmolean Museum, Oxford
(p 37)

DAVID COX (1783–1859)
Tour d'Horloge, Rouen 1829
Pencil and watercolour on paper
343 × 257
T00977 (p 48)

DAVID COX (1783–1859)
Night Train c 1849
Watercolour with scratching out on paper
285 × 381
Birmingham Museum and Art Gallery
(p 50)

DAVID COX (1783–1859)
Stone Bridge, Wales c 1850s
Watercolour over black chalk on rough 'Scotch'
paper
276 × 379
Birmingham Museum and Art Gallery
(p 49)

ALEXANDER COZENS (c 1717–1786)
Landscape with Fir Trees
Pencil and watercolour on paper
133 × 171
N01359 (p 15)

JOHN ROBERT COZENS (1752–1797)
*The Entrance to the Valley of the Grande Chartreuse
in Dauphiné* c 1783
Watercolour on paper
262 × 377
The Visitors of the Ashmolean Museum, Oxford
(p 19)

JOHN ROBERT COZENS (1752–1797)
The Gulf of Salerno c 1790
Watercolour on paper
371 × 537
T00984 (p 18)

JOSHUA CRISTALL (1767–1847)
Beach Scene at Hastings c 1808
Watercolour on paper
184 × 302
T01851 (p 34)

JOHN DOWNMAN (c 1750–1824)
Tree Trunk near Albano 1774
Pen and watercolour on paper
539 × 387
Private Collection (p 23)

ANTHONY VANDYKE COPLEY FIELDING
(1798–1855)
Cader Idris from the Barmouth Sands 1810
Watercolour on paper
213 × 654
T00988 (p 32)

JOHN FLAXMAN (1755–1826)
Procession of Ancient British Priests c 1793
Pen and wash on paper
482 × 697
The Syndics of the Fitzwilliam Museum,
Cambridge
(p 35)

THOMAS GIRTIN (1775–1802)
The White House at Chelsea 1800
Watercolour on paper
298 × 514
N04728 (p 29)

JAMES HOLLAND (1800–1870)
Rotterdam 1845
Pencil, watercolour and body colour on paper
432 × 298
T01002 (p 44)

EDWARD LEAR (1812–1888)
*Substructure of the Palace of Septimus Severus,
Palatine* c 1838
Watercolour on paper
184 × 330
N02743 (p 31)

JOHN FREDERICK LEWIS (1805–1876)
Study for 'The Proclamation of Don Carlos' c 1835–40
Watercolour and body colour over pencil on
paper
444 × 630
The Visitors of the Ashmolean Museum, Oxford
(p 51)

JOHN LINNELL (1792–1882)
Tatham's Garden, Alpha Road, at Evening 1812
Watercolour on paper
102 × 125
T04139 (p 9)

JOHN BAPTIST MALCHAIR (1729–1812)
St Barnabus, Oxford, from the Artist's Window 1782
Watercolour and pencil on paper
268 × 346
The Visitors of the Ashmolean Museum, Oxford
(p 6)

JOHN HAMILTON MORTIMER (1740–1779)
Monsters c 1770s
Pencil and black ink and watercolour on paper
421 × 285
The Visitors of the Ashmolean Museum, Oxford
(p 7)

WILLIAM JAMES MÜLLER (1812–1845)
The Avon, 4 1834
Watercolour on paper
292 × 441
N02323 (p 40)

SAMUEL PALMER (1805–1881)
Villa d'Este, Tivoli 1838
Water and body colour over pen and ink on paper
335 × 504
The Visitors of the Ashmolean Museum, Oxford
(p 47)

WILLIAM PARS (1742–1782)
On the Tessin near Poleggio
Watercolour on paper
247 × 349
Private Collection (p 18)

NICHOLAS POCOCK (1741–1821)
Waterfall: Pistyll Ghaedra
Pencil and watercolour on paper
295 × 295
Private Collection (p 22)

DAVID ROBERTS (1796–1864)
Ronda, Spain 1834
Watercolour on paper
235 × 330
T01011 (p 43)

THOMAS ROWLANDSON (1757–1827)
Landscape, Isle of Wight c 1782
Pen and ink and watercolour on paper
200 × 276
T01014 (p 7)

JOHN RUSKIN (1819–1900)
View of Bologna 1845 or 1846
Pen and wash on paper
343 × 489
N03507 (p 27)

JOHN RUSKIN
Aiguille Blaitière 1849
Pencil, pen and wash on paper
250 × 360
The Syndics of the Fitzwilliam Museum,
Cambridge (p 27)

JONATHAN SKELTON (c 1735–1759)
The Ponte Molle and the Tiber in Flood 1758
Watercolour and body colour over pencil and ink
on paper
369 × 530
The Visitors of the Ashmolean Museum, Oxford
(p 14)

FRANCIS TOWNE (1739 or 1740–1816)
The Bay of Naples c 1781
Pen and ink with wash on paper
236 × 317
The Visitors of the Ashmolean Museum, Oxford
(p 21)

JOSEPH MALLORD WILLIAM TURNER
(1775–1851)
Traeth Mawr, with Y Cnicht and Moelwyn Mawr?
1799
Pencil and watercolour on paper
545 × 764
D03647 (p 38)

JOSEPH MALLORD WILLIAM TURNER
(1775–1851)
A Ravine on the Pass of St Gothard 1802
Gouache, pencil and watercolour on paper
318 × 475
D04627 (p 38)

JOSEPH MALLORD WILLIAM TURNER
(1775–1851)
Benson (or Bensington), near Wallingford c 1805–6
Pencil and watercolour on paper
259 × 371
D05917 (p 41)

JOSEPH MALLORD WILLIAM TURNER
(1775–1851)
*Castel dell'Ovo, Naples, Capri and Sorrento in the
Distance* 1819
Pencil and watercolour on paper
255 × 404
D16093 (p 39)

JOSEPH MALLORD WILLIAM TURNER
(1775–1851)
Rouen, West Front of the Cathedral c 1832
Gouache and watercolour on paper
140 × 194
D24674 (p 45)

JOSEPH MALLORD WILLIAM TURNER
(1775–1851)
Venice: Open Air Theatre 1833
Gouache and watercolour on dark brown paper
226 × 292
D24674 (front cover)

JOSEPH MALLORD WILLIAM TURNER
(1775–1851)
Funeral at Lausanne 1841
Pencil and watercolour on paper
235 × 337
D33526 (p 46)

JOHN VARLEY (1778–1842)
Sunrise from Cader Idris 1804
Watercolour on paper
285 × 488
Private Collection
(not illustrated)

CORNELIUS VARLEY (1781–1873)
Evening at Llanberis 1805
Watercolour on paper
200 × 238
T01710 (p 24)

PETER DE WINT (1784–1849)
Westmorland Hills, bordering the Ken c 1830–35
Watercolour on paper
146 × 635
N03496 (p 33)

PETER DE WINT (1784–1849)
Cliveden on Thames c 1812
Watercolour on paper
297 × 467
The Syndics of the Fitzwilliam Museum,
Cambridge
(p 30)

PETER DE WINT (1784–1849)
Study of Trees at Lowther c 1839
Watercolour on paper
460 × 293
The Syndics of the Fitzwilliam Museum,
Cambridge
(p 23)

TWENTIETH CENTURY WORKS

AVIGDOR ARIKHA (b 1929)
Tubes of Paint in their Drawer 1985
Pastel on paper
499 × 329
T04939 (p 8)

GÜNTHER BRUS (b 1938)
Untitled 1960
Black poster paint on buff paper
1257 × 900
T04927 (p 15)

GÜNTHER BRUS and ARNULF RAINER
No, Daphne, No! 1984
Pencil on paper
577 × 402
T05212 (p 30)

PAUL KLEE (1879–1940)
They're Biting 1920
Watercolour over oil-colour drawing on paper
311 × 235
N05658 (p 8)

BRICE MARDEN (b 1938)
I 1986
Green painting ink over pencil with blood stains
on paper
470 × 1005
T04938 (p 35)

PABLO PICASSO (1881–1973)
Bottle of Vieux Marc, Glass, Guitar and Newspaper
1913
Papier collé and pen and ink on blue paper
467 × 625
T00414 (p 34)

ARNULF RAINER (b 1929)
Rain 1951
Wax crayon on paper
859 × 612
T03906 (p 10)

DAVID SMITH
Don Quixote 1952

MARK ROTHKO (1903–1970)
Untitled (Brown and Grey) 1968–9
Acrylic on paper
1730 × 1235
T04149 (p 25)

DAVID SMITH (1906–1965)
Don Quixote 1952
Lithograph with hand colouring on paper
453 × 605
P77434 (above)

WOLS (Alfred Otto Wolfgang Schulze)
(1913–1951)
Untitled c 1944–45
Black ink, watercolour and gouache on paper
92 × 135
T04845 (back cover)

FURTHER READING

Herbert Read, W G Archer and Robert Melville, *40,000 Years of Modert Art; A Comparison of Primitive and Modern*, London, Institute of Contemporary Art, 1948

Iolo A Williams, *Early English Watercolours*, Kingsmead Press, Bath (reprint), 1970

Michael Clarke, *The Tempting Prospect; A Social History of English Watercolours*, London, 1981

Graham Reynolds, *English Watercolours*, 2nd. ed., London, 1988

Kirk Varnedoe, *A Fine Disregard; What makes Modern Art Modern*, New York, 1990

ISBN 1 85437 077 4

Published by order of the Trustees for
the exhibition 'Original Eyes: Progressive
Vision in British Watercolour 1750–1850'
22 May – 4 August 1991

Published by Tate Gallery Publications,
Millbank, London SW1P 4RG
Edited by Joanna Skipwith
Designed by Jeremy Greenwood
Colour origination and printing in
Great Britain by Balding + Mansell plc,
Wisbech

ILLUSTRATION CREDITS

Photographs have been provided by the
photographic departments of the
following museums

The Ashmolean Museum, Oxford: pp. 6,
7 lower, 14, 19, 21, 23 lower left, 37,
47, 52
Birmingham Museum and Art Gallery:
pp. 49, 51
The Fitzwilliam Museum, Cambridge:
pp. 23 upper right, 27 lower, 30 lower,
35 lower
The Paul Mellon Centre for Studies in
British Art: pp. 18 upper, 23 upper left
Tate Gallery, London, for all works in
the Tate Gallery collection

Works by Picasso, Rainer, Smith and Wols
have been reproduced by permission of
© DACS, London, 1991
The work by Pollock has been reproduced
by permission of © ARS, New York, 1991
The work by Rothko has been reproduced
by permission of © Kate Rothko-Prizel
and Christopher Rothko, ARS, New York,
1991